DAUGHTER OF THE

ATHENEUM BOOKS FOR YOUNG READERS • An imprint of Simon & Schuster Children's Publishing Division • 1230 Avenue of the Americas, New York, New York 10020 • Text © 2024 by Belen Medina Cabot • Illustration © 2024 by Natalia Rojas Castro • Book design by Lauren Rille © 2024 by Simon & Schuster, LLC • All rights reserved, including the right of reproduction in whole or in part in any form. • ATHENEUM BOOKS FOR YOUNG READERS is a registered trademark of Simon & Schuster, LLC. Atheneum logo is a trademark of Simon & Schuster, LLC. • Simon & Schuster: Celebrating 100 Years of Publishing in 2024 • For information about special discounts for bulk purchases, please contact Simon & Schuster Special Sales at 1-866-506-1949 or business@simonandschuster.com. • The Simon & Schuster Speakers Bureau can bring authors to your live event. For more information or to book an event, contact the Simon & Schuster Speakers Bureau at 1-866-248-3049 or visit our website at www.simonspeakers.com. • The text for this book was set in Gazpacho. • The illustrations for this book were rendered digitally. • Manufactured in China • 0224 SCP • First Edition • 10 9 8 7 6 5 4 3 2 1 • Library of Congress Cataloging-in-Publication Data • Names: Cabot, Belen Medina, author. | Castro, Natalia Rojas, illustrator. • Title: Daughter of the light-footed people : the story of indigenous marathon champion Lorena Ramírez / Written by Belen Medina ; Illustrated by Natalia Rojas Castro. • Description: First edition. | New York, New York : Atheneum Books for Young Readers, [2024] | Includes bibliographical references. | Audience: Ages 4–8 | Audience: Grades 2–3 | Summary: "From the copper canyons of Mexico her swift footsteps echo. Clip clap, clip clap. Experience a 60-mile run with indigenous athlete Lorena Ramírez, who captured the world's attention when she won an ultramarathon in Mexico wearing a skirt and rubber sandals—the traditional clothes of the Rarámuri, 'the light-footed people.'"—Provided by publisher. • Identifiers: LCCN 2023005409 (print) | LCCN 2023005410 (ebook) | ISBN 9781665931427 (hardcover) | ISBN 9781665931434 (ebook) • Subjects: LCSH: Ramirez, Lorena, 1995-—Juvenile literature. | Indigenous peoples—United States—Biography—Juvenile literature. | Women runners—United States—Biography—Juvenile literature. | Runners (Sports)—United States—Biography—Juvenile literature. | Marathon running—Mexico—Juvenile literature. • Classification: LCC GV1061.15.R36 C33 2024 (print) | LCC GV1061.15. R36 (ebook) | DDC 796.42092 [B]—dc23/eng/20230306 • LC record available at https://lccn.loc.gov/2023005409 • LC ebook record available at https://lccn.loc.gov/2023005410

LiGHT-FooTeD PeoPLE

by Belen Medina   illustrations by Natalia Rojas Castro

The Story of Indigenous
MaRaThoN CHaMPioN LoReNa RaMíRez

Atheneum Books for Young Readers | New York London Toronto Sydney New Delhi

From deep in the copper canyons
of Mexico, her swift footsteps echo.

Clip clap, clip clap.

In her well-worn huaraches cut from rubber tires,
her feet strike the ground.
She runs in a skirt sewn by her mother.

Swish, swoosh,

swish, swoosh.

With strength built from herding goats
and cows for her family
and kicking balls across miles
in games with her siblings.

Tapa tapa,

tapa tapa.

With patience built from walking for hours to buy food, drinking from waterfalls and streams on the way.

Drip,
gulp,
drip,
gulp.

Over hot, cracked earth
and rocks,

through cold,
    hard rain,

she runs.

In daylight and darkness,
crossing towering bridges,

ascending steep mountains.
Ten miles she runs.

Legs pumping,

lungs breathing,

heart beating.

Ba bump, ba bump.

Against hundreds from other countries,
she weaves to the front of the pack
without fancy gear or gadgets.

Zip zoom,

zip zoom.

She wipes the salty sweat from her squinting eyes
with a handkerchief. With a stick in hand,
she pushes off the ground as the path steepens,
birds soaring overhead, clouds coming closer.

Twenty miles she runs.

Fans taking photos,
as they do during all her races
that crisscross the globe . . .

Clap! Clap!

Mexico, Europe, the US.

Snap! Snap! Snap! Snap!

Thirty miles she runs.

"Lorena!"

"Lorena!"

Clap! Clap!

When thirst and hunger grumble,
she drinks from a bottle of water mixed with pinole,
the food that has sustained her ancestors for generations.

Now knee pain slows her to a walk.
Her muscles throb and ache.
Will she have the endurance to carry on one more step?

From somewhere deep inside,
she finds the strength
to pick up the pace.

Her muscles draw energy from the earth
with every footfall.
She inhales the life-giving force
of the oxygen around her.

Forty miles she runs.

Quiet as a deer.

Quick as a rabbit.

Graceful as a gazelle.

She thinks of the finish line,
of her family,
and of her community,
not of giving up.

Fifty miles she runs.

As a proud daughter of the Rarámuri,
"the light-footed people,"
unstoppable Lorena runs . . .

and runs . . .

After sixty miles, she crosses the finish line!
Her family stretches out their arms to greet
her with love, pride, and celebration . . .

This daughter
of the light-footed people.

About Lorena

María Lorena Ramírez (born 1995) is an ultramarathon runner belonging to the Rarámuri Indigenous people—sometimes called the Tarahumara—of Chihuahua, Mexico, who run as a way of life. In 2017, she made international news when she won the Ultra Trail Cerro Rojo, a fifty-kilometer (thirty-one-mile) race, beating five hundred other runners from twelve countries. What caught people's attention was not only that she won but what she was wearing. Lorena wore huaraches (sandals made of rubber tires) and a brightly colored skirt, the traditional clothes of Rarámuri women.

Since then, Lorena has participated and placed highly in many other races around the world, including ultramarathons as long as a hundred kilometers (around sixty miles). Fans have sent her modern, high-tech running shoes—but she prefers to wear her huaraches, feeling like she will slip otherwise. "I don't think I'm going to use them [running shoes]," she once said. "The people wearing them are always running behind me."

The Rarámuri are known for being excellent endurance runners. In their language, "rarámuri" means "the light-footed people" or "those who run fast." Lorena and her family live in a remote region of northwest Mexico, far from any other people and surrounded by mountains and canyons. She runs in the Barranca del Cobre, or Copper Canyon, so named because of the copper-like colors of its walls. It is four times bigger than the Grand Canyon. The Rarámuri have called this place home since before Spain colonized Mexico.

Life is not easy for the Rarámuri. Lorena and her family must walk or run for hours through the canyon to buy food and supplies. This is one way she built her endurance. She also built up her stamina by herding the family's goats and cows, as well as playing a Rarámuri running game where players kick a ball across miles.

The Rarámuri still eat their traditional foods, such as corn, beans, and cow and goat products. One of the Rarámuri's most important foods is pinole, a traditional drink made from ground corn and spices. Sometimes this is all Lorena drinks to sustain her while running.

Farming is not always enough to support Rarámuri families, and there are few other jobs in the canyon. Many of the Rarámuri, including Lorena, help their families make a living by winning races. Lorena's father and a few of her siblings are also runners; they often enter races together, and sometimes Lorena's relatives even manage to outrun

her! Running marathons, as extreme as it seems, is what the Rarámuri have to do to support themselves and preserve their community.

Lorena is a quiet, determined woman who says a lot with few words. Because her family didn't have enough money to send her to school, she only speaks the Rarámuri language and never learned Spanish. In interviews with reporters, her brother Mario translates for her. Mario describes her as "strong, admirable, kind, serious, and direct."

When she runs, Lorena says she only thinks of one thing: getting to the finish line. When asked why she runs, she says, "Because I'm good at it." She runs in traditional clothes to show her pride in her people. As she said in one interview, she runs "to give value to the Rarámuris" and in traditional dress "to be representative of what refuses to die." She is proud of who she is and where she comes from, and although she's appeared in newspapers and magazines all over the world, she is still a humble person who does not appear to be changed by fame.

Lorena's persistence is what I find most inspiring about her. Whether she wins or loses a race, she stays determined and never compromises who she is.

To my boys, Henry and Nate,
who I hope will be as persistent in chasing
their dreams as Lorena —B. M.

For Marge —N. R. C.

SOURCES

Rulfo, Juan Carlos, dir. *Lorena, la de pies ligeros (Lorena, Light-Footed Woman)*. 2019; Mexico: No Ficción. Netflix.

McDougall, Christopher. *Born to Run: A Hidden Tribe, Superathletes, and the Greatest Race the World Has Never Seen*. New York: Knopf Doubleday Publishing Group, 2011.

"Mexican Tarahumara woman wins 50km race wearing sandals." *BBC News*, May 23, 2017. https://www.bbc.com/news/world-latin-america-40006985.

Terrell, Jordan C. "Born to Run? How Raramuri Runners Dominate Ultra-Marathons in Sandals | NBC Left Field." NBC News. Streamed on August 24, 2018. YouTube video, 6:47. https://www.youtube.com/watch?v=25DE-lrO3qM.

Coppel, Eugenia. "How a Tarahumara woman won a Mexican ultramarathon in sandals." *El País*. May 24, 2017. https://english.elpais.com/elpais/2017/05/24/inenglish/1495618559_311854.html.

Esparza Loera, Juan. "Life on the run is more than a tradition for Rarámuris like Lorena Ramírez." *The Fresno Bee*. December 14, 2021. https://www.fresnobee.com /vida-en-el-valle/deportes/article256480586.html.